Days That Changed the World

THE FIRST

"TEST-TUBE BABY"

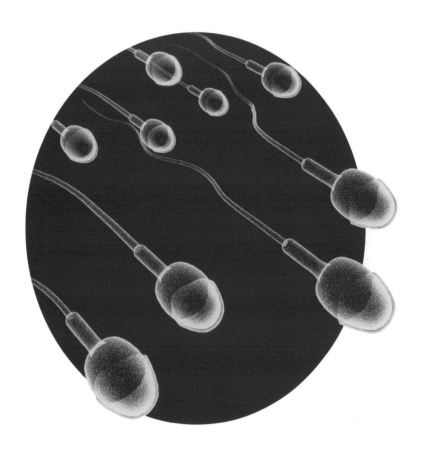

Fiona Macdonald

WORLD ALMANAC® LIBRARY

Please visit our web site at: www.worldalmanaclibrary.com
For a free color catalog describing World Almanac® Library's
list of high-quality books and multimedia programs,
call 1-800-848-2928 (USA) or 1-800-387-3178 (Canada).
World Almanac® Library's fax: (414) 332-3567.

Library of Congress Cataloging-in-Publication Data available upon request from publisher.
Fax (414) 336-0157 for the attention of the Publishing Records Department.

ISBN 0-8368-5567-1 (lib. bdg.)
ISBN 0-8368-5574-4 (softcover)

This North American edition first published in 2004 by
World Almanac® Library
330 West Olive Street, Suite 100
Milwaukee, WI 53212 USA

We would like to thank: Tall Tree Ltd, Lizzy Bacon, and Ed Simkins for their assistance.

World Almanac® Library editor: Carol Ryback
World Almanac® Library cover design: Steve Schraenkler

Photo Credits:
t=top, b=bottom, c=center, l=left, r=right, OFC=outside front cover
Alamy: 14, 31b, 43b. CORBIS: 17b, 18-19, 28t, 36, 37, 39, 42br. Hulton Archive: OFC, 4bl,
 22tl, 29 (both), 30, 31t, 43t. Mediscan: 6-7, 11, 22-23, 26, 27t. PA Photos: 34, 40, 43cr.
Science Photo Library: 1, 5r, 16, 18, 21 (both), 24 (both), 25bl, 27b, 28cr, 35b, 42tl.

Printed in the USA

1 2 3 4 5 6 7 8 9 08 07 06 05 04

CONTENTS

Some ancient South American cultures crafted fertility pipes, whistles, and charms like this one for women who hoped for increased fertility.

Just before midnight on July 25, 1978, a healthy baby girl made medical history when she was born at Oldham General Hospital in Lancashire, in northern England. Her name was Louise Joy Brown. She was the very first baby — anywhere in the world — born as the result of an experimental new treatment designed to help infertile couples produce children. The treatment's scientific name is "In-vitro fertilization," or "IVF," but most people called Louise the "Test-Tube Baby."

Louise Brown, the world's first test-tube baby, celebrated her second birthday with a party.

Before the development of the IVF technique, infertile couples — couples without children — simply and often sadly accepted their inability to have a family. Most societies believed that the female half of the couple was the one with some sort of problem.

These women were labeled "barren" and shunned by society. Scientific developments in the nineteenth and twentieth centuries led to a better understanding of human reproduction. By the 1960s, scientists began investigating the complex problem of infertility. A real breakthrough came in 1965, when two British doctors — Dr. Robert Edwards and Dr. Patrick Steptoe — developed a new, experimental treatment called "In-vitro fertilization."

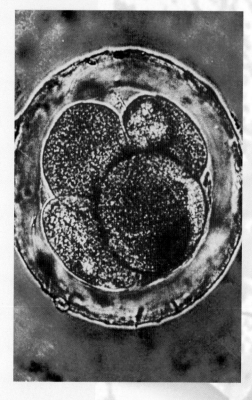

John and Lesley Brown of Bristol, England, volunteered for the IVF program as soon as they could. Within one year of trying the new technique, Louise was born. Her birth also marked the end of many years of painstaking research by a pioneering medical team that began working with infertile couples in 1966.

Until Mrs. Brown gave birth to Louise, none of the earlier IVF attempts were successful.

IVF treatment involves removing ripe eggs from a woman and fertilizing them with a man's sperm in the laboratory. The eggs are then implanted into the woman's body. The goal is for at least one implanted egg to begin dividing and growing into what will eventually become a human baby. Some very early stages of cell division in an egg are visible in this electron micrograph.

Hundreds of thousands of babies have been born since 1978 thanks to IVF. The technique also led to a dramatic increase in the number of multiple births, such as twins, triplets, quadruplets, quintuplets, and even septuplets!

While the IVF technique seemed shocking when Louise Brown was born in 1978, it was just one of many exciting medical advancements — along with organ transplants, gene therapy, and cloning — that occurred in the second half of the twentieth century. These breakthroughs revolutionized our understanding of how the human body works. The IVF success led to new treatments for infertility and a greater knowledge of its causes.

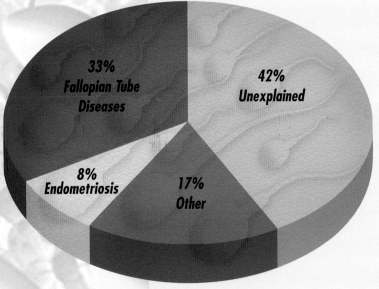

Current researchers possess a greater understanding of infertility than ever before. Fallopian tube problems are the most common reason for infertility, but in more than 40 percent of cases, doctors cannot pinpoint a specific cause for the condition.

42%
Unexplained

33%
Fallopian Tube Diseases

8%
Endometriosis

17%
Other

Today, researchers acknowledge many other causes of infertility — from alcohol and drug abuse to eating disorders and old age. Conditions such as diabetes and kidney disease, and environmental factors, such as exposure to pollutants, may also cause infertility. Medical research also led to new ways of controlling fertility, such as the contraceptive pill.

The IVF technique that produced Louise Brown and many thousands more "test-tube" babies after her, brought might "customize" their children by choosing height or eye color. Further advances in research posed other possibilities, such as cloning — producing an identical offspring from only one parent. While scientists have successfully cloned several different animals, such as frogs, sheep, monkeys, pigs, and mice, no scientifically documented cloning of a human being is currently on record. In fact, most countries throughout the world outlaw human cloning.

great happiness to their parents and gave hope to couples all around the world who wanted children. Fertility-related research also contributed to the discovery of new treatments for several other medical conditions.

As with many important scientific discoveries, IVF also raised some important and difficult questions for individuals and societies. These questions involved ethical dilemmas such as the possibility of creating "designer babies" — where parents

After only twenty-one weeks, a human fetus assumes a recognizable form and can hear and open its eyes. It also finds its mother's voice soothing.

Frenchman Claude Vorilhon, now known as "Rael" (left), leads the Raelian Movement — a cult that believes life began in space. Raelians also claim they created the world's first cloned baby, "Eve," in 2002, and plan to clone more children in the future. No medical researcher or scientist ever proved that the Raelians cloned a human.

Couples get married or set up home together for a variety of reasons. Some reasons are emotional — people fall in love or develop companionships. Other reasons are practical — in some countries, moving in with a partner is the only culturally acceptable way of leaving the parental home. But many couples agree that their lives and future are incomplete without children. However, for some people making this step is not so easy, and they experience problems producing children of their own.

Attitudes towards children vary from century to century and from culture to culture, but one thing has never changed: becoming a parent brings joy and fulfillment. A happy family enjoys the day (below) in this painting by French impressionist Renoir.

Fulfillment

Becoming a parent creates a great sense of fulfillment, joy, and responsibility. Many men and women feel that raising a happy, healthy family is the most important activity in their lives. Certain communities give extra respect to those who are parents. In fact, some people in Arabic-speaking societies change their names when their first son is born. They become known as "Abu" (father of) or "Umm" (mother of), followed by the baby's name.

Security

Many countries value children for an additional reason: They are useful! Children run errands, care for younger brothers and sisters, and sometimes go to work. Parents often consider their offspring "insurance" – a way of providing comfort and security in old age. In most African and Asian cultures, children are expected to care for their aged parents.

LOVED and Valued

Although some people choose not to have children, the vast majority decide to raise a family. Over 2,500 years ago, a Hebrew poet wrote: *"Happy is the man who has his quiver full of children."* Around 150 B.C., Roman noblewoman Cornelia praised her sons, saying, *"These children are my jewels."*

Name and fame

Rich and powerful people often pass on their land, wealth, or titles to future generations. Rulers throughout history hoped to produce sons who would reign after them — although few could match the example of Pharaoh Ramses II of ancient Egypt (who reigned from 1279 to 1213 B.C.). He fathered more than one hundred children by many different wives.

Reproduction

In the twentieth century, scientists suggested an additional reason why so many men and women feel that they simply must, if possible, produce a child. The theory is that our genes — the chemical code inside cells that determines what we look like and how we grow — are "selfish." Genes seek to live forever by passing themselves on from generation to generation. Before pregnancy can start, and a baby can be born, a woman must conceive. Conception is a complex and delicate process. But it is also very common — countless billions of babies have been conceived since the first humans evolved. Conception is often known as "an everyday miracle." But what is it, and how does it happen?

Conception

Conception is a three-stage process that takes between seven and ten days to establish itself inside a woman's body. It involves the production of an egg and some sperm, the fertilization of the egg, and the implantation of the fertilized, fast-growing egg into the lining of the woman's uterus, or womb.

> "I have often wished for the blessing of motherhood… With it, and through the varied experiences that accompany it, I could perhaps have achieved something better than that which I have… until now."

Swedish opera star Jenny Lind, one of the most famous and successful women of her day, wrote about her thoughts on motherhood in 1849.

In some of the world's poorer countries, parents carry their children to the fields. When they are old enough, the children assume a portion of the work.

FERTILITY AND INFERTILITY

FERTILITY *facts*

- A woman's ovaries contain around 400,000 immature eggs. Only about five hundred eggs ever mature enough to accept fertilization by sperm.
- Sperm determine whether the fertilized egg develops into a female or a male offspring.
- It takes sperm about forty-five minutes to reach the fallopian tubes.
- Sperm stay alive and ready to fuse with an egg in the fallopian tubes for about three days.

Pregnancy affects women physically and emotionally.

Eggs and sperm

Most adult humans produce special cells designed for reproduction. Women produce eggs, and men produce sperm. Eggs and sperm are made and stored in the adult sex organs — two testes in men, two ovaries in women — that mature when a child reaches puberty (usually in early teenage years). Each egg or sperm contains only half the number of chromosomes (genetic information) needed to create a normal body cell.

To survive, the egg and sperm must fuse (join together), linking the two sets of chromosomes. When this happens, they create a new cell containing enough genetic information to become a new life.

Fertilization

Eggs and sperm normally join together during sexual intercourse. Sperm produced by the man's testes swim along the woman's vagina, into the uterus, and then enter the fallopian tubes. There, only one sperm fuses with one egg. The sperm must burrow through the egg's outer surface so that its chromosomes combine with those belonging to the egg. This process is called fertilization.

Division

As soon as an egg is fertilized, cell division begins. This process continues rapidly. After 72 hours, the fertilized egg's cells have divided 32 times, and the egg contains a total of 64 cells. When it reaches this stage, the egg begins to travel down the fallopian tubes to the uterus. This journey takes as long as seven days.

Implantation

While the egg travels, tiny finger-like projections grow around its outer edge. These projections burrow into the uterine lining and help the fertilized egg draw nourishment from the lining's rich blood supply. This process is called "nidation" or "implantation." Conception is now complete. A pregnancy has begun. A mother can look forward to having her baby.

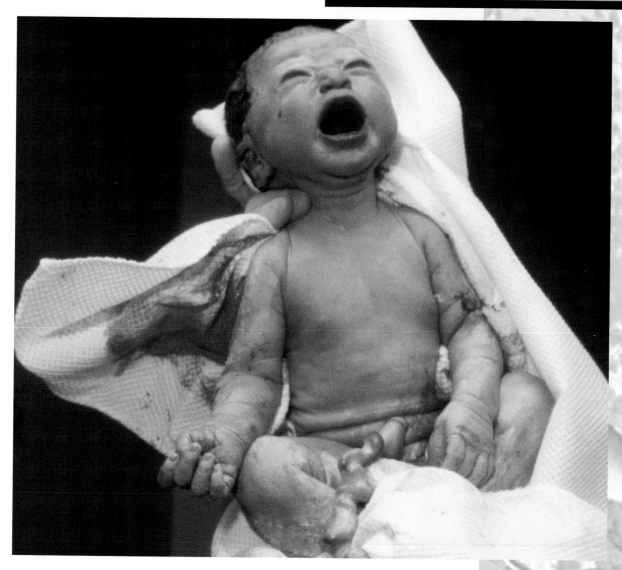

Infertility

Not all people who want children can have them naturally. Doctors estimate that as many as one in six couples is infertile. These couples may try for many years before the woman becomes pregnant (conceives) — or she may fail to conceive at all. In the past, people developed superstitious beliefs to explain why someone did not have children. Today, we understand and can identify the many scientific reasons behind infertility .

Parents never forget the experience of holding their baby for the first time. This baby's umbilical cord is still attached. Doctors will tie the umbilical cord in two places and cut it between the ties to separate the baby from its placenta. The umbilical cord eventually dries up and falls off. The spot where it once connected baby and mother is called the umbilicus. It is also known as the navel, or "belly button."

OVULATION

Men produce roughly 200 million sperm daily, but a woman ovulates — produces an egg ready for fertilization — only about twelve times a year. About two weeks before a woman's period, one of the ovaries releases a ripened egg. It travels to the fallopian tube, where it lives for an average of twelve hours. If not fertilized by a sperm, the egg dies.

FERTILITY AND INFERTILITY

Queen Anne Boleyn, Henry VIII's second wife, fell victim to the prejudiced beliefs about pregnancy common during the sixteenth century and long afterward. Henry VIII's blood type probably interfered with his wife's ability to produce a second child.

Supernatural

Many regard the birth of a baby as a miraculous event. So it is not surprising that, in the past, people looked for magical reasons, such as bad luck, witchcraft, or even a punishment from God to explain why a couple did not produce children.

Charms and rituals

To protect themselves from evil influences that might prevent them from becoming pregnant, women wore magic amulets or carried lucky charms. They engaged in complicated rituals designed to increase their fertility. The rites often involved symbols of new life, such as eggs. They recited prayers, gave offerings, and made pilgrimages to holy places asking their god or gods to send them the gift of a child.

The woman's fault?

Now we know that either the man or the woman can be infertile, but in the past infertility was almost always considered the woman's fault. It was very shameful for a woman to be labeled "barren," and meant that she had failed in her most important life's duty — to have children.

Punishing "failure"

In many countries, a husband could divorce a wife if she failed to give birth. King Henry VIII, who ruled England from 1509 to 1547, is famous for marrying six times in the hope of producing a male heir to the throne. His second wife, Anne Boleyn, had a daughter, but then gave birth to a stillborn (dead) son. Historians today believe that Anne and Henry's differing blood types caused the death of the baby (*see p. 13, Rhesus Factor box*). Because her baby died, Anne Boleyn was accused of witchcraft, put on trial, found guilty, and beheaded!

GIFT *from God?*

People from all different faiths perceive fertility as a gift from a higher power. For example, one sixteenth-century book that teaches about the Roman Catholic faith states: *"Married people, having received the gracious gift of fertility from God, which He does not give to everybody, must give humbly Him thanks every time a child is born."* Other religious organizations hold similar views today. They oppose abortion and contraception, and preach the belief that only God should decide who will have a child.

In the past, couples who could not produce their own children found other ways of having a family. They adopted children (became their legal parents) or fostered them (agreed to care for them for a period of time). Oftentimes, barren couples would take in orphans (children whose parents had died), foundlings (children who were abandoned at special hospitals), or children born to ill, overworked, or unwed mothers.

THE RHESUS *factor*

Human blood contains many different chemicals, including a certain protein called the "rhesus factor" or "Rh factor" found on red blood cells. People with this protein are Rh positive, while those without it are Rh negative. If an egg from an Rh-negative woman is fertilized by sperm from an Rh-positive man, the unborn child's blood will be Rh positive as well. However, the mother's immune system will recognize this Rh difference and form antibodies (killer cells) to fight against it. This is not a problem until a second pregnancy occurs. Then antibodies can seriously damage an unborn baby, or any future babies with Rh-positive factor blood.

This ancient South American fertility charm would have been carried by a woman hoping to increase her fertility.

FERTILITY AND INFERTILITY

Most adoptive or foster parents have a very rewarding relationship with their children, who grow up in a loving family environment.

Given away

Until about 1900, couples without children in Europe or the U.S. might ask a relative to give them a child to bring up as their own — especially if the relative had several children. In many cultures, such as those in West Africa and the Caribbean, it was also common for parents to send some of their children to be fostered with relatives who cared for them, raised them, and provided them with schooling or taught them useful skills.

No choice

Often, these children were greatly loved and given many advantages. But they were very rarely consulted, or even asked to consent, to a move that would dramatically change their lives. Being adopted or fostered meant that these children lost close contact with their entire family, including parents, brothers, and sisters for a long time — sometimes forever.

WORTH *the Effort*

In most countries, becoming an adoptive parent is a long process. Couples undergo detailed psychological examinations, and social workers investigate their private lives. But many adoptive parents feel that these procedures are all worthwhile, for the sake of adopting a longed-for child.

Happy together

Unfortunately, there were sometimes cruel and abusive adoptive or foster parents and unhappy, badly treated children — just as in all other families. However, on the whole, adoption and fostering arrangements have provided millions of infertile couples and their adopted and fostered children with happy and full family lives.

New ideas

Ideas about adoption changed in the late twentieth century. Experts believed it was better for children to stay with their natural parents whenever possible and offered help and support to families facing problems. Improved methods of birth control — especially the contraceptive pill — meant that fewer "unwanted" babies were born. Changing social attitudes made it perfectly acceptable for an unmarried woman — or man — to raise a child by themselves. At the same time, well-meaning infertile couples

from wealthy countries who adopted babies born in poor or war-torn nations were criticized for taking children away from their homeland and their heritage.

"Something must be done"

Many couples without children became less willing to accept infertility as "bad luck" or "God's punishment." These couples convinced doctors and researchers to resolve the problem of infertility. Women in wealthy countries wanted to try any new procedures that would help them carry a baby to term. Unlike women in the past or women in poor countries today — where pregnancy and giving birth could seriously endanger the mother's life — most late-twentieth-century and twenty-first-century women do not share those fears.

Societal changes of the 1960s decreased the impact of religious teachings on marriage, pregnancy, and fertility. In particular, changes occurred in society's attitudes toward unmarried mothers. New government benefits also improved the situation for single mothers.

"Your pink, healthy face will turn sickly green… your eyes will lose their sparkle. Your belly will swell and you will have indigestion and pains in your side. Your back will ache. You will look pale and ill … no longer beautiful … and everything you eat will make you feel sick. You will be unable to sleep at night, because you will worry so much about the pain of giving birth."

— A thirteenth-century European priest, encourages young women to stay virgins and avoid pregnancy

In the past, doctors wanting to treat infertility faced a major problem. The female reproductive system is hidden deep inside the body, making very difficult to observe. For centuries, no one really understood women's bodies, and religious leaders in many countries forbade dissection (the cutting up of dead people) to investigate. Then, around 1500, doctors inspired by Renaissance ideas that encouraged exploration and scientific inquiry began to examine real bodies, and published their findings for others to study.

Andreas Vesalius (1514–64) founded the modern science of anatomy. His beautifully illustrated books were the first to show accurate details of the human body.

1537–1543 Flemish doctor Andreas Vesalius, a professor at the university of Padua, Italy, published *Six Anatomical Pictures* and *On How the Human Body is Made*. Unlike earlier doctors who gained their knowledge about the insides of the human body from studying animals and the writings of ancient wise men, Vesalius made his discoveries by dissecting humans. His books marked the start of a new approach to the study of anatomy and disease.

CUTTING UP *criminals*

Vesalius dissected corpses of executed criminals for his investigations. On one occasion, he even robbed a wayside gibbet — a gallows — and carried away the body hanging there for further study.

1561 Italian anatomist Gabriello Fallopius, who followed Vesalius as a professor at Padua, published *Anatomical Observations*. In it, Fallopius described in detail the tubes that carry eggs from

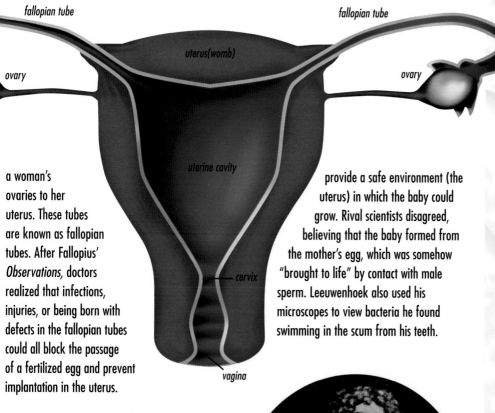

fallopian tube

fallopian tube

uterus(womb)

ovary

ovary

uterine cavity

cervix

vagina

A woman's ovaries alternate producing one mature egg per month. The egg travels down the fallopian tube to the uterus. If this egg comes into contact with a man's sperm, the fertilized egg implants itself into the uterine lining and begins developing into a baby. When the baby is ready to be born, the strong uterine muscles push it out during labor.

a woman's ovaries to her uterus. These tubes are known as fallopian tubes. After Fallopius' *Observations*, doctors realized that infections, injuries, or being born with defects in the fallopian tubes could all block the passage of a fertilized egg and prevent implantation in the uterus.

provide a safe environment (the uterus) in which the baby could grow. Rival scientists disagreed, believing that the baby formed from the mother's egg, which was somehow "brought to life" by contact with male sperm. Leeuwenhoek also used his microscopes to view bacteria he found swimming in the scum from his teeth.

1677 Dutch scientist Anton van Leeuwenhoek, a pioneer microscope maker, was able to magnify items more than two hundred times. The first to see sperm, he called them "human larvae" (larvae are tiny grubs that grow into insects). Like many people at the time, he thought that babies developed from sperm alone, and a mother's role in pregnancy was simply to

Leeuwenhoek not only researched fertility, but also made important discoveries about bacteria.

"It is a truth too well known, that mothers and their children are daily, if not hourly, destroyed (such is the practice of midwifery in our days) by ignorant wretches ... a pack of young boys and old superannuated [retired] washerwomen, who are so impudent and inhuman as to ... practice, even in the most difficult cases."

— An "expert" male midwife hoping to encourage new birthing techniques in London 1785

SPERM *matters*

On average, a man produces about 20 billion sperm every month, and around 400 million enter a woman's body each time a couple has sexual intercourse. Each sperm is tiny — far too small to see with the naked eye. Sperm were first seen under early microscopes in the seventeenth century. But it was only in the nineteenth century that scientists finally understood the role sperm play in conception.

UNDERSTANDING INFERTILITY

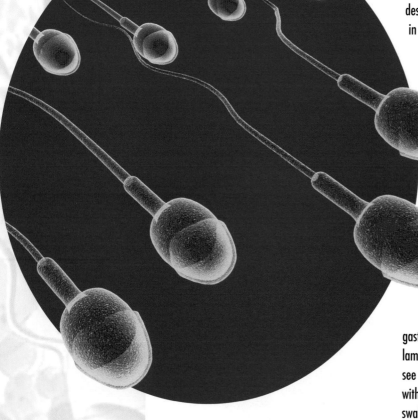

A scanning electron microscope (SEM) — one of the most powerful microscopes available — reveals tiny sperm in incredible detail.

1700–1800 New discoveries about female anatomy improved midwifery techniques. This made childbirth less dangerous for many women. It also helped prevent infertility caused by injuries received while giving birth. But it took many years for the latest scientific discoveries to reach traditional female midwives and inexperienced male doctors.

1828–1837 Estonian scientist Karl Ernst von Baer published *Developmental History of Animals*. He explained for the first time how ovaries worked in humans and other mammals. He reached many of his conclusions after carefully studying his cook's pet dog! Von Baer was also the first to describe how a fertilized egg grows in the early stages of conception.

1843 British doctor Martin Barry discovered how a human sperm and egg fuse at the moment of fertilization. His observations made it clear that male and female cells play equally important roles in conception.

1868 A team led by German doctor Adolf Kussmaul invented the gastroscope, a pipe fitted with a tiny lamp and lenses that allowed him to see inside the human stomach — with the help of a fairground sword-swallower! Other doctors used this invention to develop the laparoscope, a tube inserted through a tiny cut in the abdomen. The laparoscope allowed them to examine reproductive organs in great detail. Today, fiber-optic endoscopes are made of bundles of glass fibers that transmit light. They are flexible, and can "see" all around and even inside organs.

LESS FERTILE *in old age*

For thousands of years, people have recognized that young men are more fertile than older ones. Around 1000 B.C., an Egyptian scribe recorded this traditional medical advice. *"Marry a wife while you are young, so that she may give you many children."* At that time, people did not know why older men are often less fertile than younger ones. Today, doctors think that sperm are weaker, and more likely to have defects, once a man is past fifty.

1929–1930 American scientists Edgar Allen, a zoologist, and Edward Doisy, a biologist, identified the main female sex hormone, estrogen. This causes sexual maturity and thickens the lining of the uterus so it is ready to host a fertilized egg. Allen's experiments included injecting laboratory mice with fluid from pigs' ovaries.

1934 German biochemist Adolf Butenandt discovered the second main female sex hormone, progesterone. This hormone prepares the fallopian tubes and the uterus to receive a fertilized egg, and helps the pregnancy to become established. Butenandt received the Nobel Prize in Chemistry in 1939 for his work.

Edward Doisy, Ph.D., received the 1943 Nobel Prize in Medicine for his work with vitamin K. He also conducted biochemical experiments with sex hormones.

> *"As recently as twelve years ago, very little was known about the nature of the sex hormones. Butenandt has made the first big step forward."*
>
> — A quote from the 1939 Nobel Prize awards panel when presenting Adolf Butenandt with his prize

A SIMPLE *solution*

Some men have solved their infertility problems by changing their underpants! Tight-fitting clothes hold the testes (where sperm is produced) very close to the body. This increases their temperature, which can damage sperm. Wearing looser, baggier underwear keeps the testes cooler and allows the development of healthier sperm.

UNDERSTANDING INFERTILITY

Francis Crick and James Watson, pictured here with their famous molecular model of the DNA double helix, shared the 1962 Nobel prize in physiology or medicine for their 1953 discovery of DNA.

1953 British biologist Francis Crick and American biologist James Watson discovered the double-helix structure of DNA (deoxyribonucleic acid) — the genetic material contained within the cells of all living things. Until this discovery, scientists were not precisely sure what happened when a sperm fertilized an egg. DNA showed how, in fertilization, genetic information from both parents combine to create a new and completely unique individual.

1957 Scottish doctor Ian Donald pioneered the use of ultrasound to monitor the development of an unborn baby inside the uterus. His machines create images of internal body organs using sound frequencies too high for humans to hear. These images help doctors determine whether a pregnancy is progressing normally. It is also used to examine a woman's uterus, ovaries, and fallopian tubes for any possible causes of infertility.

ECTOPIC *pregnancy*

An ectopic pregnancy occurs when a fertilized egg implants itself — but not in the woman's uterus — and starts growing. Ectopic pregnancies are very dangerous, because the growing baby (at this stage, doctors call it a fetus) can cause serious internal bleeding that may kill the mother. Ectopic pregnancies are terminated (ended) to protect the mother's life.

A color x ray reveals blocked and damaged fallopian tubes. The tube on the right (blue) is blocked near the uterus (light blue triangle).

1965 British biologist Dr. Robert Edwards researched new techniques for treating women with blocked or damaged fallopian tubes. He developed a mixture of chemicals, called a culture medium, to nourish the eggs and sperm so they could live and grow outside the body. Edwards mixed sperm with unripe eggs removed from ovaries. The technique was not successful.

1966 Dr. Edwards teamed up with Dr. Patrick Steptoe, a British gynecologist (a doctor specializing in women's reproductive health). Dr. Steptoe had experience using laparoscopes to investigate infertility. A laparoscope is a long, thin surgical instrument with a light and a fiber-optic lens. Doctors insert the laparoscope through a very small cut in the skin and muscle to see inside the body. Steptoe and Edwards used a laparoscope to collect ripe eggs from women's ovaries. They mixed the eggs with sperm in a laboratory dish so that the sperm could fertilize the eggs. To ensure that their patients produced a good supply of ripe eggs, Edwards and Steptoe gave women powerful hormones to stimulate the ovaries.

1972 Edwards and Steptoe placed some eggs that were fertilized in their laboratory inside the uteruses of women with damaged fallopian tubes. They wanted the fertile eggs to implant in the uterus and develop into babies. In 1975, Briton Marlene Platt was the first to become pregnant using this method. Unfortunately, the procedure ended in an ectopic pregnancy (*see box page 20*) and the implanted, fertilized egg was removed.

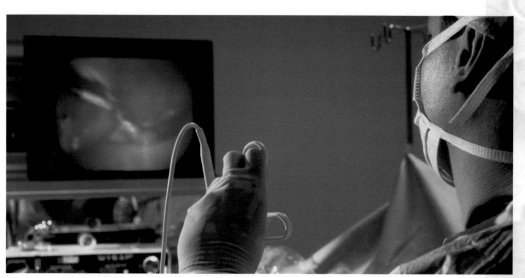

Robert Edwards and Patrick Steptoe were close to making a major scientific breakthrough for years. Their ultimate goal was the birth of the world's first baby conceived through in-vitro fertilization.

A NEW HOPE FOR PARENTHOOD

John Brown is the father of the world's first test-tube baby, Louise Joy Brown.

Lesley and John Brown were an ordinary couple. They lived in Bristol, a city in western England, where Mr. Brown was a railway worker. They never expected to break records, participate in pioneering experiments, or become famous. However, the Browns' extraordinary, risky decision made medical history and gave hope to millions of would-be parents throughout the world.

NEW SCIENCE · 1975

Like many young couples, the Browns decided they wanted to have a baby, but Lesley could not become pregnant. Doctors later discovered that she had problems with her fallopian tubes, — one of the most common causes of infertility. However, the Browns were trying to have a baby at a time when medical science was making great strides in many fields. For example, the first successful heart transplants in humans occurred only eight years earlier, in 1967.

VISIT TO OLDHAM · 1976

News of Dr. Edwards' and Dr. Steptoe's experimental "IVF" treatment (see Views) was just becoming known. The Browns' doctor suggested that the couple consult the researchers. Dr. Steptoe's laboratory was at Oldham General Hospital, in northern England. His equipment there included a special incubator that kept eggs at the correct temperature after removal from the woman's body. Other experienced doctors, nurses, and midwives at Oldham also worked with patients enrolled at the infertility clinic. With the hope that this might be their chance to have a baby at last, the Browns visited Oldham to see Dr. Steptoe.

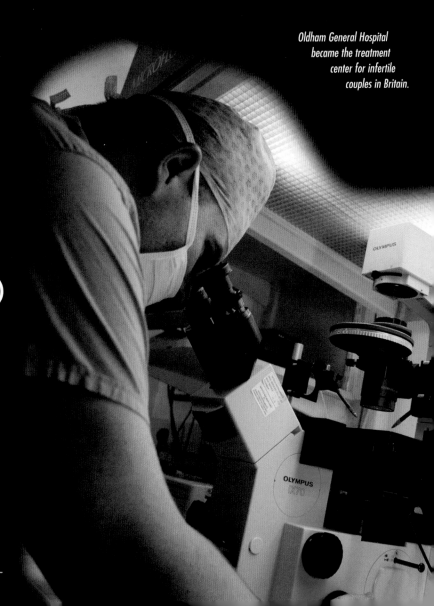

Oldham General Hospital became the treatment center for infertile couples in Britain.

VIEWS *from the ground*

> *"It was a very hard time as human nature makes you look for someone to blame and I didn't have anyone, it was my body. It was even harder to cope with the fact that I was responsible for putting my husband through this daily torture."*
>
> — a woman describes the emotional distress caused by her infertility

> *"For around five weeks prior to our first attempt, I was having daily injections. I found it mentally quite difficult to put a needle into myself, but I only had to think, 'Well, if you don't, you won't have a baby,' and I managed."*
>
> — a woman describes part of her IVF treatment

> *"There is quite a lot of anxiety till you find out from the lab how many embryos have fertilized. ... sometimes, even though the eggs and sperm look excellent, there may be a total failure of fertilization."*
>
> — an infertility specialist describes the frustration

THE RIGHT PATIENTS?

1977

Before IVF treatment began, Dr Steptoe needed to ensure that the Browns were physically and emotionally suitable patients for his experimental program. The Browns had to be able to produce healthy eggs and sperm. They also had to be prepared to cope with the stress of lengthy medical treatments, painful injections and multiple blood tests, intimate examinations, powerful drug treatments, and constant monitoring by doctors and nurses. Steptoe also warned the Browns that there were no guarantees of success. After nearly eighty attempts and one tragic termination, there was still no baby.

The Browns took powerful drugs and hormones during treatment to help boost their chances of making a baby.

Lesley and John Brown agreed to proceed with the IVF treatment. Even today — more than twenty years after the first IVF treatments — infertile couples find this a difficult decision. In the late 1970s, it was a brave step into the unknown.

Blood samples helped determine whether IVF would work for the Browns.

A NEW HOPE FOR PARENTHOOD

THE PLAN `1977`

Dr. Edwards and Dr. Steptoe made detailed plans for treating Mrs. Brown. After many failures, they decided to change the procedure. They decided against giving Mrs. Brown hormones to stimulate her ovaries into producing several ripened eggs. Instead, they would monitor her menstrual cycle and "harvest" just one ripe egg when it was naturally ready for release from her ovary.

Nurses regularly checked Lesley Brown's temperature to determine when to harvest an egg from her.

EGG COLLECTING `11:11:11`

By monitoring Mrs. Brown's menstrual cycle, the doctors calculated the date for when one of her eggs would be mature enough to use. After anesthetizing her, Dr. Steptoe made a small cut in Mrs. Brown's abdomen. Gently, he pushed a laparoscope through this opening and examined her ovaries. As hoped, he saw a ripe egg. Using the laparoscope, he collected it. Then Dr. Edwards took over and placed the egg in a glass dish. He mixed in some of Mr. Brown's sperm so that fertilization could take place. Next, he added a special culture medium (liquid) to help keep the egg and sperm alive. Finally, he placed the dish in an incubator to keep it at the same temperature as the human body: 98.6 degrees Fahrenheit (37 degrees centigrade).

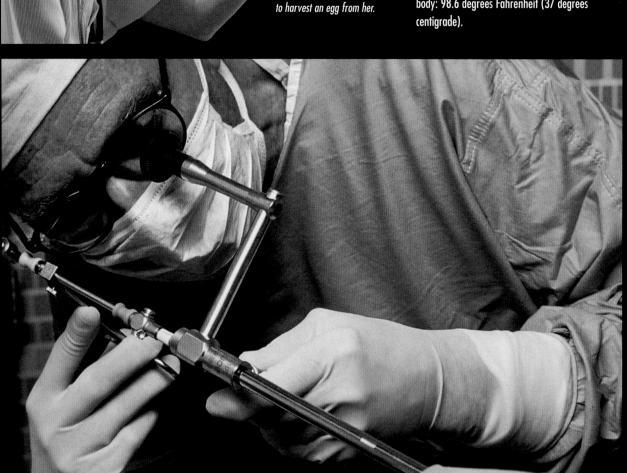

Doctors at Oldham General Hospital used a laparoscope to collect a ripe egg from Mrs Brown.

FERTILIZATION

11:11:77

Dr. Edwards checked the dish to see if the sperm had fertilized the eggs. It worked! The cells of the egg had started to divide and the embryo began growing. Genetic material from the sperm was combining with genetic material in the egg. Despite this success, the team realized it was far too soon to celebrate. The most delicate and the most risky part of the procedure lay ahead.

The fertilized egg started to divide, just as doctors had hoped.

Doctors insert a fertilized egg back into Mrs Brown.

IMPLANTING THE EGG

11:13:77

In earlier treatments, Dr. Steptoe waited four or five days after harvesting but before placing the fertilized egg (now an embryo) back inside the woman's body. This time, he and Dr. Edwards decided to put Lesley Brown's embryo back inside her body after only two-and-a-half days. A thin, flexible plastic tube carried the embryo through her vagina into the uterus. If everything went well, the embryo would implant itself in the uterine

A NEW HOPE FOR PARENTHOOD

VIEWS *from the ground*

"This period [fourteen days after the embryo is placed in the uterus] is often the hardest part of an IVF cycle for the patient, because of the suspense of waiting to find out if a pregnancy has occurred ... For many patients, these fourteen days are often the longest days of their life!'

— a physician at Oldham General

"Although my pregnancy went smoothly, it was emotionally draining ... I would have loved to have contact with ... someone who could just say that all my fears were normal, they felt the same...."

— a woman who received IVF treatment

"Every time you start [an IVF] cycle, you have to hope for the best and be prepared for the worst. Interestingly, we often find that couples going through a second IVF are much more relaxed and in control ... they are aware of all the medical minutiae and are better prepared for these."

— a physician at Oldham General

THE PREGNANCY BEGINS

If a woman conceives and becomes pregnant, levels of a hormone called HCG rise in her body. HCG levels are measured by taking a sample of blood about 10–14 days after implantation. Doctors carefully monitored Lesley Brown's hormone levels. By early December 1977, blood tests confirmed that she had conceived. This was an exciting — but anxious — time for the Browns and the entire medical team. Many other IVF treatments had failed. For the next eight months, progress of Mrs Brown's pregnancy was checked and observed, using many different techniques, such as ultrasound and amniocentesis. Everyone hoped that her pregnancy would follow a normal pattern.

A five-week-old embryo takes shape.

1-10 WEEKS

The embryo grows very fast during this stage. It changes from a shape resembling a tadpole to a more recognizable human form. Its size increases from the size of a grain of rice at week four to about 2.5 inches (6 centimeters) at week ten. All the main organs — such as brain and lungs — form, the heart begins to beat, and blood begins to flow. It has minute sex organs and tiny arms and legs — complete with fingers and toes!

11-20 WEEKS

The embryo's skeleton changes from soft, stretchy cartilage to bone. After this stage, doctors call it a "fetus." Its digestive system develops, and tiny "tooth buds" form inside its gums. By 16 weeks, its eyes can tell light from dark, and its ears can hear loud noises. It grows eyelashes, eyebrows, and fingernails. By 20 weeks, it is about 10 inches (25 cm) long and weighs about 12 ounces (350 grams). It feels, moves, and kicks.

21-30 WEEKS

The fetus's brain grows and becomes more active. After about 23–24 weeks, it can probably feel pain. By 28 weeks, its eyes are open, it has excellent hearing, and can recognize its mother's voice. The skin thickens and it looks plumper because stores of fat build up to help regulate its temperature after birth. It has regular times of sleeping and waking, and probably dreams. By 30 weeks, it is 16 inches (40 cm) long and weighs about 3 pounds (1.5 kg).

An embryo has definite features, such as arms, hands, ears, and a nose by 21 weeks.

An ultrasound image of a 32-week-old embryo displays a distinct profile.

31-40 WEEKS

The fetus now gains about 8 ounces (225 g) a week. Its lungs grow and develop so it can breathe air at birth. Its eyes can focus, its hands can grip, and its feet can make stepping movements. The fetus responds to noise and music, and it can turn its head to look around. By 40 weeks, it is ready to be born.

A NEW HOPE FOR PARENTHOOD

Dr. Edwards and Dr. Steptoe give the latest news on Mrs Brown at a press conference.

PUBLIC UNEASE

Week by week, Mrs. Brown's pregnancy progressed. She stayed healthy, and tests showed that the fetus was developing normally inside her uterus. However, when Dr. Edwards and Dr. Steptoe announced to the media that their treatment had achieved a pregnancy that was going well, the news was greeted with shock, surprise, and alarm. Many people were intrigued and impressed, but just as many were doubtful. Some worried that being outside the uterus for a few days might have harmed the egg or the fertilized embryo, and that the baby might have serious disabilities. Others warned of the dangers of "meddling with nature" or "trying to play God," and prophesied that a monster might be born.

DANGEROUS PROBLEM

Dr. Steptoe calculated that Mrs. Brown's baby was due on August 3, 1978. Everyone felt relieved and optimistic that things had gone well. Suddenly, however, problems occurred. Routine tests revealed that Mrs Brown had developed toxemia. This condition (called pre-eclampsia) can raise blood pressure to dangerously high levels. Dr. Steptoe knew that — if left untreated — it could lead to a much more serious condition, and that Mrs. Brown and her unborn baby could both die.

OPERATION

Dr. Steptoe decided that it would not be safe to allow the pregnancy to continue. He would perform an operation – called a "Cesarean section" – to deliver the baby and reduce the risk of any further problems developing. Late in the evening, Mrs. Brown was taken to the operating room, along with a camera crew. In a Caesarian section, the mother is anaesthetized and feels no pain. The doctor carefully cuts open her abdomen and then the uterus. An assistant surgeon removes the baby from the uterus and makes sure it is breathing while the primary doctor closes the opening made in the skin.

Surgeons perform a cesarean section

VIEWS *from the ground*

"I am so happy I could cry. It was just like a dream."
— Mr. John Brown

"Within five seconds of birth she let out the biggest yell you've heard a baby make."
— Dr. Edwards

"She is a beautiful baby. She's got a very small amount of hair."
— camera operator who filmed the birth of Louise Joy Brown

"I've never seen a man so excited."
— a hospital worker

"Mrs Brown, You've Got a Lovely Daughter"
— from the song of the same name, recorded by the rock group Herman's Hermits

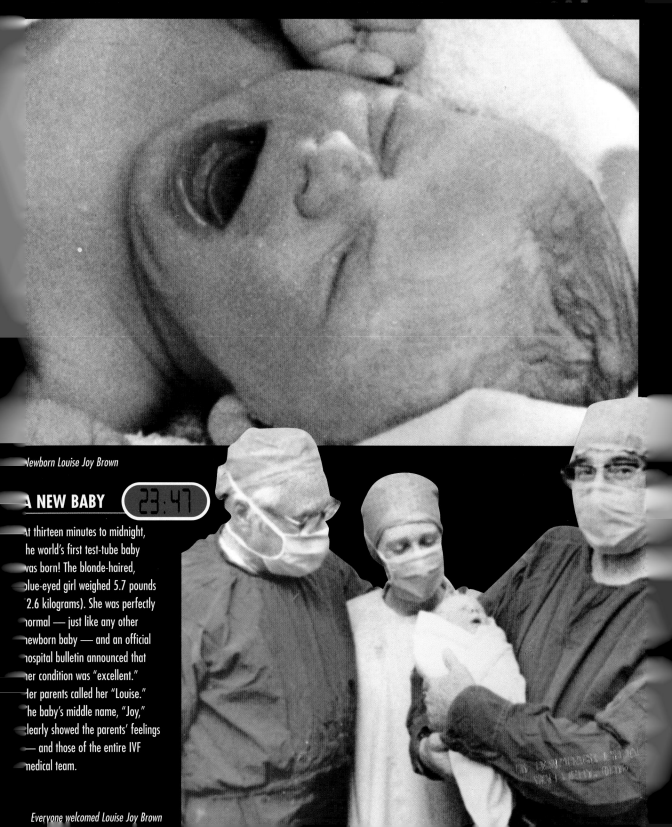

Newborn Louise Joy Brown

A NEW BABY ⏱ 23:47

At thirteen minutes to midnight, the world's first test-tube baby was born! The blonde-haired, blue-eyed girl weighed 5.7 pounds (2.6 kilograms). She was perfectly normal — just like any other newborn baby — and an official hospital bulletin announced that her condition was "excellent." Her parents called her "Louise." The baby's middle name, "Joy," clearly showed the parents' feelings — and those of the entire IVF medical team.

Everyone welcomed Louise Joy Brown

Most people who heard the news shared John and Lesley Brown's delight in the birth of their longed-awaited child. Many politicians, scientists, and media commentators also congratulated British physicians Patrick Steptoe and Robert Edwards for their pioneering research of IVF.

> In 1978, dramatic newspaper headlines all over the world announced the birth of Louise Joy Brown. The Associated Press declared her a
>
> *"...miracle child..."*
>
> Good Housekeeping magazine described the news as
>
> *"...the most extraordinary birth in human history..."*

Comfort and joy

Louise was a "miracle baby." Her birth brought new hope to millions of infertile couples all around the world as doctors learned from, and copied, the IVF techniques. For many people, even the opportunity to try IVF treatment brought tremendous comfort.

As one doctor explained, "The agony of childlessness is impossible to describe, and the joy after an infertile couple produces a child is also impossible to describe." John and Lesley Brown underwent IVF treatment for a second time to complete their family — and produced a sister for Louise, named Natalie.

Motherhood

The ability to have children is particularly important in certain traditional societies, such as India. Dr. Brij Kalyan, of the Hope Infertility Clinic in Bangalore, India, said, "IVF is the best thing that could happen to the Indian woman, who is under tremendous pressure from many quarters to conceive and produce a child to prove her womanhood." Not all women agreed. Some feminists argued that infertility should be considered a social — not a medical — problem. The feminists believed that women should be valued for themselves, not just as mothers of the next generation.

Lesley Brown proudly showed Louise to the world's media in August 1979. The healthy, normal baby reassured many that the revolutionary technique did not produce a "monster."

New uses

Some new uses for IVF techniques were fairly straightforward, such as breeding pedigree pigs or racehorses. Farmers and stock-breeders realized that IVF could be used to mate prize-winning animals from different countries without the difficulties and stresses to the animals caused by transporting valuable livestock by air or sea.

A frightening future?

Other IVF uses were more controversial. They involved experiments with genetic engineering. For example, researchers attempted to create plants that frost or insects could not harm. In the future, scientists might also try screening embryos for "defects," such as inherited diseases, before placing them back inside women's bodies. Many people feared that this might make it too easy to create "designer babies," chosen at embryo stage based on their potential strength, intelligence, or physical attractiveness.

Breakthrough

News of Louise's birth was hailed around the globe as a great breakthrough, especially by other infertility specialists. They also recognized that the techniques developed by Edwards and Steptoe for keeping eggs, sperm, and embryos alive and healthy outside the human body would be useful for many other purposes.

In an interview with Minnesota Public Radio in 1998, leading U.S. gynecologist Howard Jones declared:

"... with one procedure, suddenly it became possible to overcome a great many difficulties which seemed almost completely insurmountable prior to that."

Together with his wife, Georgeanna (also a gynecologist), Howard Jones performed the U.S's first successful IVF procedure in 1981. Research by the Jones's in the 1960s helped Dr. Edwards with some of his early fertility experiments.

Elizabeth Jordan Carr was the first test-tube baby in the United States. She was born in Norfolk, Virginia, in December 1981.

PLAYING *God?*

Some people, even radical thinkers such as British Labor politician Leo Abse, worried about where IVF treatment might lead. Abse was well-known for supporting campaigns to reform U.K. laws relating to children, divorce, family planning, and homosexuality. But in 1978, when Louise Brown was born, he commented: *"The issue is how far we play God, how far are we going to treat mankind as we would animal husbandry [breeding]."*

More than a horror story, Mary Shelley's classic novel, Frankenstein, explored the implications of science interfering with nature. The Frankenstein monster is a favorite subject of countless movies.

In 1932, British novelist Aldous Huxley published *Brave New World*. In it, he imagined a country where babies were mass-produced in factories, just like cars. They were conceived in test tubes and grown in large glass jars until they were ready to be born. The government organized all births, and babies were genetically engineered for usefulness and obedience. Natural pregnancy and human feelings such as parental love were banned. Huxley's book was his criticism of his own times. But in 1978, after the announcement of Louise Brown's birth, some people feared that Huxley's nightmare vision might come true.

Birth of a monster?

Some people compared Louise's birth to Mary Shelley's story, *Frankenstein*. Published in 1818, the book tells the story of a medical student who puts together body parts in his laboratory and creates an uncontrollable monster. Some people believed that Louise Brown was also a "monster," even though medical tests suggested she was entirely normal. They worried that she might not grow properly, that she would develop an incurable genetic disease, or that she would age quickly.

A psychic zombie?

Other people believed that the IVF procedure altered Louise Brown's mind, and gave her psychic powers. They claimed Louise could move objects simply by looking at them! One group argued that Louise's method of conception made her an "empty shell," without a soul — like a zombie.

Breaking laws

Critics argued that the IVF broke human and holy laws, and that everyone involved might be punished (by future events, or by nature) as a result. For example, the Roman Catholic church taught that unnatural ways of conceiving children was wrong, and warned that "science without conscience can only lead to man's

CARL LAEMMLE presen

FRANKENSTEIN

THE MAN WHO MADE A MONSTER

COLIN CLIVE, MAE CLARKE
JOHN BOLES BORIS KARLOFF,
DWIGHT FRYE EDWARD VAN SLOAN & FREDERIC KERR.
Based upon the
Mary Wollstonecroft Shelley Story

Adapted by JOHN L BALDERSTON
from the play by PEGGY WEBLING

DIRECTED BY ... JAMES WHALE
PRODUCED BY .. CARL LAEMMLE, JR.

A UNIVERSAL PICTURE

ruin." Psychologists argued that IVF babies might feel that there was something bizarre, abnormal or shameful about the way in which they were conceived, and that this might ruin their lives. Protesters attempted to get the U.S. Congress to ban IVF treatment altogether.

INTO THE *unknown*

Many scientists admired the medical advances of Edwards and Steptoe, but they welcomed the test-tube baby procedure with caution. Researchers felt the future of the IVF technique was unpredictable. In 1978, one genetics expert summed up their views: *"When man is fumbling at the source of life, not even a brilliant physician as Dr. Steptoe can read the consequences in advance."*

Medical fears

Medical research experts worried that without more knowledge and tighter legal controls, IVF could create serious problems. If doctors accidentally damaged eggs, sperm, or embryos in the laboratory, it might cause disabilities in the babies conceived through IVF. Also, the availability of IVF might tempt women desperate for a child to agree to new, more dangerous procedures. Scientists warned that unregulated IVF — without strict legal and ethical guidelines — could cause serious problems.

Terminator (1984) presented a future in which humans no longer controlled their own technology — which unleashed terror in the form of a half-human, half-machine, or "cyborg."

N ow, in the early twenty-first century, IVF techniques are greatly developed and improved. Doctors not only know how to manage a woman's hormones in a precise, controlled way, but also how to improve the fertilizing power of men's sperm. In-vitro fertilization is a routine medical procedure throughout the globe. While no precise figure exists, experts believe that more than one million babies have been born worldwide since 1978 thanks to IVF.

ZIFT and GIFT

Expansion of early IVF techniques led to the development of other infertility treatments, including ZIFT (Zygote Intrafallopian Transfer) and GIFT (Gamete Intrafallopian Transfer). With ZIFT, an egg fertilized in a glass dish is placed in the woman's fallopian tube, rather than her uterus. GIFT, a similar technique, places a carefully chosen egg and some selected sperm separately in a woman's fallopian tube so that fertilization takes place there. Both techniques involve major surgery for the woman. Likewise, both procedures work well, but no proof exists that either ZIFT or GIFT is more successful than IVF.

A group of IVF children and their parents gathered at "The Angel of the North" sculpture in northern England.

ROUTINE *procedure*

IVF treatment is now a routine procedure, especially in wealthy countries. In 1998, twenty years after Louise Brown's birth, a U.S. radio journalist reported: *"More than 350 American clinics perform the procedure some 40,000 times annually. An estimated 45,000 American offspring have been conceived by IVF since 1981."*

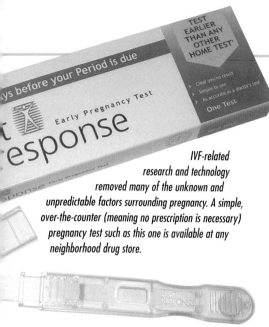

IVF-related research and technology removed many of the unknown and unpredictable factors surrounding pregnancy. A simple, over-the-counter (meaning no prescription is necessary) pregnancy test such as this one is available at any neighborhood drug store.

ICSI

In the 1990s, researchers invented another new infertility treatment, using amazingly delicate techniques to handle eggs and sperm. ICSI (Intra-cytoplasmic Sperm Injection), involves isolating just one sperm and injecting it into a woman's egg for fertilization. Many doctors hope that ICSI will become more successful than IVF, especially in cases of problems with a man's sperm.

Sharing fertility

New information learned about fertility thanks to years of experience with IVF has also helped couples who failed to have children even through this process. Women whose eggs are damaged can receive healthy ones from donors. In some countries, such as the United States, infertile women can become pregnant through implantation of donor embryos — eggs and sperm from other people and fertilized in the laboratory.

Wider uses

Close monitoring techniques such as ultrasound, developed to check the progress of IVF treatment, have also helped save the lives of many pregnant women and their unborn babies. And intensive studies of female hormones have also led to new treatments for several serious female diseases,

such as breast cancer. Since 1978, IVF has brought great joy to many families. Now that the first IVF babies are healthy adults, it appears that many of the early fears about "monster children" or "Frankenstein families" were groundless. But IVF still has many critics. Why?

High cost

IVF is very expensive. Each attempt averages between $3,000 and $5,000. In the United Kingdom and other countries with national health services, IVF treatment is not always provided by the government. In countries such as the U.S., where families rely on private health insurance, IVF insurance coverage varies by state. As a result, poor couples cannot afford fertility treatments, and the opportunity to use IVF is limited to only those rich enough to pay for it themselves.

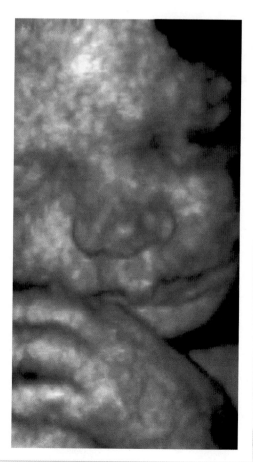

"... it is only since the breakthrough with IVF that so many couples who would have remained childless have been able to experience the natural joy of parenthood. My twins, a girl and a boy, were born healthy in February 1998 — the family I always dreamed of, they just took a bit longer than I anticipated. Ask me... what the birth of Louise Brown meant to me and I will tell you, it changed my life."

— *a British woman who experienced successful IVF treatment*

Ultrasound techniques developed from the need to monitor IVF. A probe passed over the woman's abdomen transmits an image of the fetus on to a monitor.

WORTH *every penny?*

In 1999, Britain's BBC news reported that one couple had spent about $55,500 on eleven IVF treatments before finally giving birth to twins.

Unfair?

These high costs make many people feel uneasy about spending so much money to treat infertile women when millions of mothers in poor countries suffer during pregnancy or die during childbirth from easily treatable conditions. Some people also question the practice of helping relatively rich couples have babies using expensive IVF when many young children in poor or war-torn lands are homeless, hungry, orphaned, or suffering from serious diseases. Critics argue that money used for IVF would be better spent on improved health care for these vulnerable people.

Dangerous?

Critics also claim that IVF is a dangerous procedure. In the 1970s and 1980s, doctors often placed several embryos inside a woman's uterus after IVF, hoping for an increased chance of conception. Most private fertility clinics did the same because they were under great pressure to succeed — which led to some women becoming pregnant with three or more fetuses at once. This was dangerous for the mother and her potential babies. The fetuses often died in the uterus, or were born too soon to survive. Alternatively, would-be parents sometimes asked doctors to kill some of the fetuses so that the others had a chance to live.

With so many children, such as this one in Ethiopia, suffering from famine and disease, critics of IVF question whether it is right to produce babies through such an expensive procedure.

Disabilities

If babies from these "multiple pregnancies" survived, they often had serious mental or physical disabilities. Today, many countries limit the number of embryos that can be placed in the uterus to three, and some doctors prefer to use only one or two. Recent critics of techniques such as ICSI fear that these new infertility methods could produce many babies with genetic diseases.

Ethics

As well as causing medical controversy, IVF and other fertility treatments raise larger issues about the use of scientific and medical discoveries, and their impact on human rights. People are asking questions about the purpose of love, sex, and marriage, and about the rights and duties of parents. Some view fertility treatments as a threat to civilization itself.

Painful failure

Since its beginnings, people criticized IVF for putting couples under tremendous strain. It can raise unrealistic hopes that end in cruel disappointment. It can also be physically and emotionally painful. Only twenty-two percent of all IVF treatments succeed — which means that most couples who try it experience failure, often several times. This failure may lead to depression and put a heavy strain on relationships.

British journalist Liz Tilberis (right), a former editor of Vogue magazine, believed that fertility treatments caused her ovarian cancer. She criticized people's reluctance to believe that the hormone treatments and other drugs involved in the IVF procedure are potentially harmful for many women.

WORTH *dying for?*

A few people even think that the hormone procedure used to stimulate a woman's ovaries during IVF treatment can trigger very serious diseases of her reproductive organs. For example, British journalist Liz Tilberis believed that the nine IVF treatments she had before giving birth to her sons led to her developing cancer of the ovaries, from which she died in 1999. Doctors say they can find no evidence to support her views, but research continues.

ADVANCES AND ETHICS

Many women and men feel "incomplete" if they do not produce a child of their own. Many feel they must try IVF as a "last chance" option. The fact that they have invested a great deal of time and money in it often makes them feel much worse if they are unsuccessful.

The right to a child?

Some people argue that IVF helps couples achieve their "right" to have a child. Others insist that there is no such right, but that men and women should learn to accept their childlessness with dignity. Many are horrified when women long past their natural child-bearing years become pregnant with IVF — as in the 1994 case of a 62-year-old Italian woman. But test-tube pioneer Dr. Robert Edwards welcomed the birth and said, "...the (older) ladies themselves don't think it is bad and I think (they) ... are to be supported."

This teenager suffers from cystic fibrosis, a hereditary disease that causes respiratory infections. Scientists believe that the controversial research involving embryos may one day cure his condition.

ACCEPTING *fate*

Improved medical knowledge gained through IVF research helped doctors understand many of the causes of infertility, but that does not help infertile mean and women cope with the sense of unfairness that many of them feel. They often ask, "Why me?" In 1998, London fertility treatment expert Professor Ian Craft said, "*Before IVF, people accepted their lot, because they couldn't do anything about it. Now they question it.*"

The right to life?

"Right to life" supporters often criticize IVF and other fertility treatments. They argue that life begins at conception, and that extra embryos created during IVF treatments are "murdered" when not used. Their opponents claim that life starts at a much later date — when a fetus has grown enough to survive outside the uterus — and that information gained by studying "spare" embryos may help cure many diseases.

Legal limits

States can make laws to control IVF procedures. Britain, for example, set up the HFEA (Human Fertilization and Embryology Authority) in 1991. But human feelings are often much more complicated than a lawyer's rules, and IVF techniques remain controversial. This is especially so when mistakes get made, such as in 2002 when eggs and sperm got mixed up at a British hospital and a woman gave birth to babies fathered by the wrong man. This raised perplexing questions, especially for the children. Their biological parents were known, but who should care for them, and give them love? Who was their legal guardian? — and who is the man they should they call "Daddy?"

Pressure groups, such as those opposed to abortion, sometimes lobby governments and take direct action. These groups feel that science such as embryo research threatens moral attitudes — of the family and the sanctity of life itself.

Louise Brown, the world's first test-tube baby, is now a fit, healthy adult. She owes her life to the IVF technique but, perhaps surprisingly, she is reported as saying that she would not want IVF treatment for herself. More than one million people, however, — parents, scientists and family friends — would not agree with her. Since 1978, IVF has brought joy and great satisfaction to many lives.

Mr. and Mrs. Hashimi waited to produce an embryo with a certain genetic makeup in hopes of saving their son Zain's life. This is one of the most obvious examples of how couples can benefit from having the right to choose an individual embryo.

Helping nature

IVF was shocking at first, but it is now widely accepted. We now know that the technique is usually safe for mothers and that children conceived by IVF are generally healthy. In some ways, IVF is not so revolutionary after all — it is simply helping nature. The only difference between IVF and natural conception is the place — a glass dish — where egg and sperm join together and fertilize. Once the embryo is returned to the mother's uterus, pregnancy continues naturally.

Life-saving

IVF treatments have also made many other, similar procedures possible. Some of these have saved lives. In 2002, British parents Raj and Shahana Hashmi sought legal permission to screen their embryos before going ahead with a pregnancy. They needed an embryo with a suitable tissue match for their sick son Zain, who has thalassemia, a serious blood disorder. They hope that blood cells from the umbilical cord of a correct tissue match will treat Zain's problem.

Genetic engineering

Many people feel alarmed at the possibility of changing the genetic code within embryos to create

FUTURE choices

Many people are cautiously excited about the recent breakthroughs in genetic research. The Church of England reacted with unease to the following 1995 statement by Dean Hamer of the American National Cancer Institute: *"We will soon have the power to change and manipulate human behavior through genetics."* John Habgood, the Archbishop of York, summed up the views of many when he said, *"[We must be] suspicious about improving human nature, and even more suspicious of those who think they know what improvements ought to be made."*

A DANGEROUS *race*

• In 2002, rival scientists Severino Antinori from Italy, and Panayiotis Zavos from the United States both claimed to be close to producing cloned humans.

• On December 26, 2002, members of the Raelian Movement claimed the birth of "Baby Eve," the world's first cloned human — although no independent scientist confirmed the birth (or viewed the baby).

• In February 2003, six-year-old Dolly the sheep, the world's first cloned mammal, was put to sleep. Dolly aged much more quickly than a normal sheep, and suffered from severe arthritis — a disease of old age.

"designer babies." It may soon be possible to not only engineer physical characteristics such as hair color, but also an embryo's personality! This raises many ethical and moral questions: Which behavioral traits are desired and which should be removed? And who, if anyone, should choose? Many countries currently ban genetic engineering.

Cloning

IVF treatment also led to one of the most controversial scientific achievements of the late twentieth century: cloning. A clone is a copy of just one parent, and is not produced by normal fertilization. The technique is difficult and far from perfect. It took scientists in Scotland 277 attempts to produce Dolly the sheep, the world's first cloned mammal. Most cloned animals born so far have had genetic defects. Human cloning is banned in many parts of the world.

No easy answers

In 2002, test-tube pioneer Dr. Edwards said he supported research into human cloning — but only if the process was proven to be safe. Other fertility experts disagreed. As with all important questions, there are no easy answers. We must think carefully about what we want for ourselves and what kind of society we want to create before we make this difficult decision.

Are we on the threshold of a future in which we can "choose" babies for athletic potential, mental abilities, or physical appearance?

41

1500–1784

• 1537: Flemish doctor Andreas Vesalius establishes the modern science of anatomy with his book Six Anatomical Pictures. It is the first publication to contain accurate drawings of human bones and organs. Vesalius makes his drawings and discoveries from corpses of executed criminals.

• 1561: Italian anatomist Gabriello Fallopius accurately describes a woman's fallopian tubes in his book Anatomical Observations. Doctors realize that infertility and damaged fallopian tubes are linked.

• 1677: Dutch scientist Anton van Leeuwenhoek, a pioneer microscopist, is the first to see sperm under a microscope, and calls them "human larvae." He believes that babies form only from sperm.

• 1777: An Italian priest experiments with artificial insemination of reptiles.

1785–1890

• 1785: British scientist John Hunter unsuccessfully attempts artificial insemination.

• 1828–1837: Estonian naturalist Karl Ernst von Baer pioneers the study of embryology. His book, Developmental History of Animals, is the first to explain how ovaries work in humans and animals.

• 1843: British doctor Martin Barry discovers how a human sperm and egg fuse together at the moment of fertilization. It becomes clear that both male and female cells play an equally important part in conception.

• 1868: German scientist Adolf Kussmaul invents the gastroscope (a pipe fitted with a light and lenses) for examining inside the stomach. Its invention gives rise to the laparoscope, which enables scientists to examine the sex organs in much greater detail.

• 1890: British scientist Robert Dickinson conducts secret experiments with donor sperm after condemnation by the Catholic church.

1891–1948

• 1929–1930: American scientists Edgar Allen and Edward Doisy identify estrogen, the main female sex hormone.

• 1934: German biochemist Adolf Butenandt discovers a second important female sex hormone, progesterone, which prepares the fallopian tube and uterus to receive an egg.

• 1948: A report on artificial insemination published in the British Medical Journal sparks a fierce debate in parliament. The Church of England recommends calling artificial insemination a criminal offense. The British government declares the practice "undesirable and not to be encouraged."

1949–1966

• 1953: British biologist Francis Crick and U.S. biologist James Watson construct a molecular model of DNA, opening the way to research into the genetic makeup of all living things.

• 1965: British biologist Robert Edwards experiments with different culture mediums (mixtures of chemicals) for keeping unripe eggs alive.

• 1966: Robert Edwards teams up with British gynecologist Patrick Steptoe. They use a laparoscope to remove ripe eggs from ovaries and fertilize them with sperm outside the woman's body.

1967–1977

1978–1989

1990–1992

1993–2002

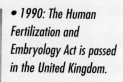

• *1990: The Human Fertilization and Embryology Act is passed in the United Kingdom.*

• *1991: The United Kingdom's watchdog organization, the Human Fertilization and Embryology Authority (HFEA), which aims to control IVF procedures, is established.*

• *1996: A Scottish sheep named Dolly is the first mammal successfully cloned after 277 unsuccessful attempts.*

• *2000: A culture using embryonic stem cells, some from "spare" embryos donated by couples who participated in IVF procedures, allow for "made-to-order" transplant tissue.*

•*1972: Edwards and Steptoe place eggs fertilized in the laboratory back inside the bodies of women with blocked fallopian tubes, hoping that the eggs will implant in the uterus. They make more than eighty unsuccessful attempts.*

• *July 25,1978: Lesley Brown gives birth to the world's first test-tube baby, Louise Joy Brown.*

• *December 1981: The first U.S. test-tube baby, Elizabeth Jordan Carr, is born in Norfolk, Virginia.*

• *January, 1992: The first successful ICSI (Intracytoplasmic Sperm Injection) pregnancy is announced. Critics warn that it may cause disabilities in babies.*

• *2002: British couple Raj and Shahana Hashimi seek the right to screen embryos before going ahead with a pregnancy, hoping to produce a baby with the correct tissue to provide cord blood to save the life of their son.*

• *1975: British woman Marlene Platt is the first to conceive by the new infertility treatment known as IVF. However, the pregnancy is ectopic and must be terminated.*

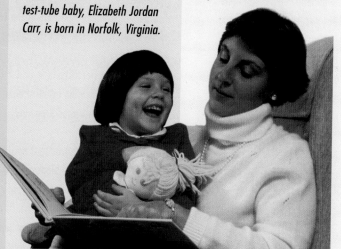

• *August, 2002: Rival scientists Severino Antinori from Italy and Panayiotis Zavos from the U.S. both claim to be close to producing cloned humans.*

• *November, 1977: British couple Lesley and John Brown begin IVF treatment after hearing of the work of Edwards and Steptoe. Lesley Brown conceives after an egg fertilized with her husband's sperm is placed in her uterus.*

• *1988: The first pregnancies are achieved as a result of GIFT — a technique that places eggs and sperm separately inside the fallopian tubes for fertilization.*

• *July 1994: Sixty-two-year-old Italian Rosanna della Corta gives birth to a son, Riccardo, after IVF treatment under the direction of Dr. Severino Antinori.*

• *December, 2002: An organization called the Raelian Movement claims to have produced the world's first cloned human — "Baby Eve." However, no independent scientist has confirmed the legitimacy of the claim, or even seen the baby.*

amniocentesis the procedure that involves taking a sample of fluid surrounding the fetus to assess its condition during pregnancy.

anatomy the branch of biology or medicine that deals with the structure of bodies or plants.

artificial insemination the fertilization of an egg with sperm by methods other than through sexual intercourse.

Cesarean section an operation to deliver a baby by cutting open the mother's abdomen while she is under general anesthetic and removing the baby directly from her uterus.

cloning making an exact copy of an organism "asexually" — without normal fertilization.

conception the fertilization of an egg by a sperm that is complete once the egg implants itself in the uterine lining.

DNA (deoxyribonucleic acid) the genetic material contained within the cells of all living things. DNA governs cell growth and passes genetic information from one generation to the next.

ectopic pregnancy a pregnancy where the fertilized egg implants and starts to grow outside the uterus. An ectopic pregnancy often ends spontaneously or is surgically terminated because the growing baby can cause internal bleeding that endangers the mother.

embryo an unborn offspring during the first eight weeks after conception. Once an egg is fertilized by sperm and starts to grow, it is considered an embryo.

fetus the name given to an unborn, developing offspring eight weeks after conception.

fertilization the joining of a single sperm with a ripe egg, either inside the fallopian tubes or outside the woman's body — if she is undergoing IVF treatment.

egg the female reproductive cell, also called an ovum. Ovaries produce ripe eggs about every twenty-eight days.

fallopian tubes ducts through which eggs travel from the ovaries to the uterus. Fertilization takes place in the fallopian tubes. The egg then moves down to the uterus for implantation.

genetic engineering the artificial manipulation of genes contained within the cells of living things. Genetic engineering techniques may allow parents to select only those embryos without defects or embryos with particular characteristics. Research into cells taken from embryos may enable doctors to produce "genetically engineered" tissue made to order for transplant surgery.

GIFT (Gamete Intrafallopian Transfer) a technique where an egg and some sperm are placed separately in a fallopian tube, in hopes that fertilization will occur.

gynecology the branch of medicine that deals with diseases and disorders of women, especially of the female reproductive system. A gynecologist is a doctor who specializes in this field.

HFEA (Human Fertilization and Embryology Authority a watchdog organization established in 1990 to regulate and control IVF practices in the United Kingdom.

hormone a chemical produced by a body gland or organ that is released directly into the bloodstream, which causes a response in or affects the activity of another gland or organ. The two main female hormones are estrogen, which causes women to become sexually mature, and progesterone, which readies the fallopian tubes and uterus to receive a fertilized egg. In some IVF treatments, women are injected with hormones to stimulate their ovaries into producing several ripened eggs.

ICSI (Intracytoplasmic Sperm Injection) an infertility treatment developed using IVF techniques. It involves isolating one sperm and injecting it into a woman's egg so that the two may fuse and fertilize. This treatment may help couples conceive if the infertility problem is caused by problems with the man's sperm.

implantation (also called "nidation") the attachment of a fertilized egg to the lining of the uterus.

infertility the inability to conceive and produce a baby.

in-vitro fertilization an infertility procedure that involves the removal of a ripe egg from a woman's body for mixing with sperm in a shallow glass dish for fertilization. The fertilized egg is then returned to the woman's body in hopes of implantation. "In-vitro" means "in glass" in Latin.

laparoscope a tube-shaped fiber-optic instrument that allows doctors to see inside the body through a small incision in the abdominal wall. Doctors use a laparoscope to remove ripe eggs from the ovaries of a woman undergoing IVF treatment.

ovaries the pair of female reproductive organs that produce eggs and female sex hormones. The ovaries take turns producing one ripe egg each month. During IVF treatment, a ripe egg is removed directly from an ovary using a laparoscope.

ovulation the process in which a woman produces a ripened egg that can be fertilized. About 12 times each year, a ripened egg is released from her ovaries about 14 days before her period and stays there stays for about twelve hours in the nearest fallopian tube, where it dies unless fertilized by sperm.

rhesus factor (Rh factor) any of several proteins present on the surface of red blood cells that cause a severe reaction in the fetus if it has a blood type different from that of the mother.

semen the liquid made in the testes that contains sperm.

sperm the male sex cells. Sperm are made in two glands called testes. Each sperm has a flagellum (tail) that enables it to swim towards the egg in the woman's uterus.

testes the two male reproductive glands that make sperm.

test-tube baby popular name given to babies born by mothers who have received IVF treatment. Actually, the egg and sperm are fertilized in a shallow glass dish instead of a test tube.

ultrasound procedure a diagnostic tool that uses sound waves to create a "picture" of what is going on inside someone's body.

uterus the muscular female reproductive organ that houses and nourishes the fetus during pregnancy (also called the "womb").

ZIFT (Zygot Intrafallopian Transfer) an infertility treatment that involves placement of a fertilized egg directly into a woman's fallopian tube.

FURTHER INFORMATION

BOOKS

Biomedical Ethics. Terry O'Neill (Gale Group)

Classic Cases in Medical Ethics: Accounts of Cases That Have Shaped Medical Ethics. Gregory E. Pence (McGraw-Hill)

Fertility Technology: The Baby Debate. Kara Williams (Rosen)

Genetics. Discovery Channel School Science. Universes Large and Small (series). (Gareth Stevens)

Genetic Engineering: The Cloning Debate. Debbie Stanley (Rosen)

Test Tube Babies: In-Vitro Fertilization. Science at the Edge (series). Ann Fullick (Heinemann Library)

Test Tube Baby. Science on the Edge (series). Jenny Tesar (Blackbirch Marketing)

The Reproductive System. Body Focus: The Science of Health, Injury and Disease (series). Steve Parker (Heinemann Library)

WEB SITES

www.dnaftb.org/naftb/
DNA from the beginning. Hit enter, then click the animation button at the bottom for a series of pages on how a creature becomes a male or a female.

www.nationalgeographic.com/ngkids/9909/dna/stage7.html
Learn how Dolly the sheep was cloned.

www.factmonster.com/ipka/A0906923.html
The Female Body/The Reproductive System. Read about the rites of passage for different cultures around the world.

www.nationalgeographic.com/ngkids/9909/dna/intro.html
Discover how cloning works.

http://gsic.genetics.utah.edu/units/cloning/
Scroll through a series of questions about cloning.

www.timeforkids.com/TFK/magazines/story/0,6277,93229,00.html
Read the story of Dolly the sheep.

www.ornl.gov/TechResources/Human_Genome/elsi/cloning.html
Find quick links to cloning facts and frequently asked questions.

www.sciam.com/article.cfm?articleID=0002AB9E-F4AA-IC72-9B81809EC588EF21&pageNumber=1&catID=2
Discover how cloning may help endangered species.

www.brainpop.com/health/growthanddevelopment/genes/index.weml?&tried_cookie-true
Watch a cartoon about genetics.